KOOKAMONGA

Zayde Berger

This book is dedicated
in loving memory
of Henry Berger
1909 - 1960

One day not so very long ago, Zayde Berger decided to go for a walk in his favorite forest. The name of the forest was "Kookamonga." He always wore his favorite hat when he went to the forest.

Zayde brought along his dog named Skinny Boy. Zayde and Skinny Boy had many friends in Kookamonga.

Along with Skinny Boy, Zayde would stop to talk with all of his friends.

Skinny Boy loved running in Kookamonga.

He would run around the trees with the bees that gathered their honey.

The bees would take the honey to the flowers in the Garden of Flowers.

One special flower that Zayde Berger and Skinny Boy liked was a flower named Dancing Flower.

Whenever they saw her, Dancing Flower's petals would be blowing in the wind.

She had special powers that could make you all better when you were hurt.

Skinny Boy also liked to run around a big beautiful pond named The Royal Fishing Pond. There were special fish in the pond. All of the fish were very beautiful.

Zayde Berger's favorite fish was named the Golden Throated Silver Fish.

One day, just before they got to The Royal Fishing Pond, Zayde heard a very loud cry.

Right in front of him was a very big elephant.

Zayde said, "Why are you crying Mr. Elephant?"

The Elephant said that he had this very big stick caught in his foot.

Zayde took a look at it and pulled the big stick right out of the elephant's foot.

After that Zayde Berger named the elephant Stick'n the Foot.

Zayde said to Stick'n the Foot, "We better get you to The Royal Fishing Pond."

At the pond, the Golden Throated Silver Fish helped clean out Stick'n the Foot's foot.

Then they all went to the Garden of Flowers so that Dancing Flowers' special healing powers would make Stick'n the Foot's foot feel all better.

Now, Stick'n the Foot was all better and when Zayde and Skinny Boy would go to Kookamonga for a walk, Stick'n the Foot was always there waiting for them.

Guess what happened next? After Stick'n the Foot went home, Zayde turned around and he could not find Skinny Boy anywhere. Zayde called out his name, but Skinny Boy was no where to be found. Zayde was very upset.

Zayde decided to go back to the Garden of Flowers to look for him there. Dancing Flower said that she had not seen Skinny Boy.

Then, Zayde thought that it would be a good idea to see if Skinny Boy had gone back to the Royal Fishing Pond. The Golden Throated Silver Fish told Zayde that she had not seen Skinny Boy.

All of Skinny Boy's friends were starting to worry about him. Zayde walked around Kookamonga calling out for Skinny Boy. No answers were heard.

Zayde decided to take a rest so that he could think about what to do next. While he was thinking about Skinny Boy, Zayde Berger looked down and standing right in from of him was his friend Stanley the Skunk.

Stanley the Skunk had beautiful stripes of black and white fur. There was something very different about Stanley. Can you guess what it was? WHEW, he smelled terrible! Stanley said that all skunks smell like that when they are afraid of something.

Zayde always kept food with him when he rested in Kookamonga. Zayde had a peanut butter and jelly sandwhich and Stanley had a handful of nuts and berries that Zayde brought along with him. Zayde made sure that all of his animal friends would get a treat from him.

Zayde asked Stanley if he had seen Skinny Boy. Stanley said he was sorry but he hadn't seen him. After awhile, Zayde told Stanley that he was going to continue looking for Skinny Boy in Kookamonga.

As he was walking, Zayde saw his good friend Mori the Moose. He had very big antlers. Do you know what antlers are? They are big horns that sit on the head of a moose. I think it must be very hard to carry around those horns all day. Don't you?

Zayde asked Mori the Moose if he was hungry. Mori was always looking for something good to eat. Just like Stanley, Mori also likes different fruits, nuts and berries. Zayde asked him if he wanted some nuts and berries to eat. This made Mori very happy.

Mori had been walking around the playground in Kookamonga because he loved watching the children play.

Zayde Berger also loved watching the children play on the playground. Zayde took his grandchildren to the playground many times. His favorite thing to do was to push his grandchildren on the swings and watch them go down the sliding board. He also liked watching the kids on the see-saw.

Zayde asked Mori if he had seen Skinny Boy. Mori told him that he heard a dog barking near the tree that Ollie the Owl was sitting. Zayde got so excited. He thanked his friend Mori and off he went to see if the barking dog was Skinny Boy.

While Zayde was walking to the tree where Ollie the Owl was sitting, he started thinking about all of the fun that he had with Skinny Boy.

He remembered Skinny Boy and Stick'n the Foot's adventures.

He remembered, Dancing Flower at the Garden of Flowers.

He remembered The Golden Throated Silver Fish at the Royal Fishing Pond.

He remembered Stanley the Skunk and Mori the Moose.

Zayde rushed to the tree where Ollie the Owl was sitting.

With his big eyes, Ollie the Owl was sitting on the tree branch looking at all of the animals that lived in Kookamonga. There were so many animals that Ollie couldn't even count them all. Ollie asked Zayde if he would like to take him to find Skinny Boy. Zayde was very excited. Ollie spread out his wings, and started to fly. He flew over all of the beautiful places in Kookamonga. Zayde had to run really fast to keep up with Ollie the Owl.

With the help of Ollie, Zayde found Skinny Boy. They were both so happy to see each other that they started jumping up and down! All of the animals were very happy that Zayde found Skinny Boy safe and sound.

Zayde Berger was so happy to find Skinny Boy that he decided to have a party with cake and balloons to celebrate Skinny Boy's safe return.

Zayde Berger believed that all of his children, grandchildren and great grandchildren and all children of the world would like to think about Kookamonga and that they would always be able to visit it whenever their parents said it was ok.

www.ingramcontent.com/pod-product-compliance
Lightning Source LLC
Chambersburg PA
CBHW060809290526
45792CB00005BA/1581